Healthy Mediterranean Diet Meal Plan

The Essential Guide breakfast, Lunch, Dinner, Snacks, Dessert Recipes for a Healthy Lifestyle

By

Mary Schulte

Contents

CHAPTER EIGHT

FREQUENTLY ASKED QUESTIONS

CONCLUSION

Introduction

The Mediterranean diet is often hailed as one of the healthiest diets in the world, with numerous studies showing its effectiveness in promoting overall health and reducing the risk of chronic diseases. This diet is based on the traditional eating patterns of countries surrounding the Mediterranean Sea, such as Greece, Italy, Spain, and Morocco. The diet emphasizes whole, minimally processed foods, with an emphasis on plant-based foods, healthy fats, and lean proteins.

A healthy Mediterranean diet meal plan can provide a wealth of health benefits, including reducing the risk of heart disease, stroke, and certain types of cancer. This eating pattern has also been shown to improve blood sugar control, promote weight loss, and improve overall mood and cognitive function.

In this essential guide to a healthy Mediterranean diet meal plan, you'll find a wide range of delicious and nutritious recipes for breakfast, lunch, dinner, snacks, and dessert. These recipes are designed to be easy to follow and incorporate a variety of flavorful ingredients that are typical of the Mediterranean diet. From savory egg dishes to fresh salads to hearty soups, there is something for everyone in this meal plan.

Whether you're looking to improve your overall health, lose weight, or simply enjoy delicious and nutritious meals, this healthy Mediterranean diet meal plan is a great place to start. By following this eating pattern, you can enjoy all the benefits of the Mediterranean diet while also satisfying your taste buds and enjoying a diverse range of delicious foods. So, get ready to embark on a delicious and nutritious culinary journey that will leave you feeling healthier, happier, and more energized than ever before!

Chapter One

What is the Mediterranean Diet?

The Mediterranean diet is a way of eating that is inspired by the traditional dietary patterns of countries surrounding the Mediterranean Sea, such as Greece, Italy, and Spain. It is not a strict diet plan, but rather a flexible and balanced approach to food that emphasizes whole, unprocessed foods and healthy fats.

The Mediterranean diet is rich in fruits, vegetables, whole grains, legumes, nuts, and seeds, and includes moderate amounts of fish, poultry, eggs, and dairy. Red meat and processed foods are limited, and saturated and trans fats are minimized.

In addition to its focus on wholesome foods, the Mediterranean diet is also characterized by social and cultural practices that promote mindful eating and enjoyment of food. Meals are often shared with family and friends, and cooking and eating are seen as pleasurable activities.

Research has shown that the Mediterranean diet is associated with numerous health benefits, including a reduced risk of heart disease, stroke, type 2 diabetes, and certain types of cancer. It may also help with weight management, cognitive function, and longevity.

The Mediterranean diet has gained popularity in recent years, and has been promoted by health experts and organizations as a healthy and sustainable way of eating. It is not a short-term or restrictive diet, but rather a long-term lifestyle choice that can improve overall health and well-being.

History and Origins of the Mediterranean Diet

The Mediterranean diet has a rich history and originates from the dietary habits of people living in the Mediterranean basin. The diet was first studied by an American scientist, Ancel Keys, in the 1950s. Keys was interested in studying the health of people living in different regions of the world, and he noticed that people in Mediterranean countries had lower rates of heart disease and longer life expectancies compared to people in other parts of the world.

Keys conducted a study known as the Seven Countries Study, which looked at the dietary habits and health outcomes of people in seven different countries, including Italy, Greece, and Yugoslavia. The study found that people in these countries had a diet rich in plant-based foods, such as fruits, vegetables, whole grains, and legumes, and consumed moderate amounts of fish and olive oil.

The term "Mediterranean diet" was coined by Walter Willett, a professor of epidemiology and nutrition at Harvard School of Public Health, in the 1990s. Willett and other researchers recognized the health benefits of the Mediterranean diet and began to promote it as a healthy way of eating.

Today, the Mediterranean diet is considered one of the healthiest dietary patterns in the world, and it has been recognized by organizations such as the World Health Organization and the American Heart Association. The diet has also been designated as a UNESCO Intangible Cultural Heritage, recognizing its role in promoting social and cultural practices related to food and health.

Key Components of the Mediterranean Diet

The Mediterranean diet is characterized by several key components that make it a healthy and balanced way of eating. These components include:

1. Plant-based foods: The Mediterranean diet emphasizes the consumption of fruits, vegetables, whole grains, legumes, nuts, and seeds. These foods are rich in vitamins, minerals, fiber, and antioxidants, and provide a wide range of health benefits.

2. Healthy fats: The Mediterranean diet includes healthy fats, such as olive oil, nuts, and fatty fish. These fats are rich in monounsaturated and polyunsaturated fatty acids, which have been shown to improve heart health and reduce inflammation.

3. Moderate amounts of dairy, poultry, and eggs: The Mediterranean diet includes moderate amounts of dairy, poultry, and eggs. These foods provide protein and important nutrients such as calcium and vitamin D.

4. Limited red meat and processed foods: The Mediterranean diet restricts red meat and processed foods since they are high in saturated and trans fats and have been associated to an increased risk of heart disease, diabetes, and cancer.

5. Herbs and spices: The Mediterranean diet emphasizes the use of herbs and spices to flavor food, rather than relying on salt and processed condiments. This helps to reduce sodium intake and adds important antioxidants and anti-inflammatory compounds to meals.

6. Social and cultural practices: The Mediterranean diet emphasizes social and cultural practices related to food, such as sharing meals with family and friends, cooking from scratch, and enjoying food in a mindful and relaxed way. These practices promote a healthy relationship with food and can contribute to overall well-being.

Overall, the Mediterranean diet is a flexible and balanced approach to food that emphasizes wholesome, unprocessed foods and healthy fats. It has been associated with numerous health benefits and is considered one of the healthiest dietary patterns in the world.

Health Benefits of the Mediterranean Diet

The Mediterranean diet has been associated with numerous health benefits, supported by a growing body of scientific research. Some of the key health benefits of the Mediterranean diet include:

1. Reduced risk of heart disease: The Mediterranean diet has been shown to lower the risk of heart disease by reducing levels of LDL (bad) cholesterol and triglycerides, improving blood pressure, and reducing inflammation.
2. Improved brain function: The Mediterranean diet has been associated with better cognitive function, including memory and attention, and a reduced risk of neurodegenerative diseases such as Alzheimer's.
3. Lower risk of certain cancers: The Mediterranean diet may reduce the risk of certain cancers, such as breast, colorectal, and prostate cancer, due to its high content of fruits, vegetables, and other plant-based foods.
4. Improved weight management: The Mediterranean diet has been shown to help with weight management and reduce the risk of obesity, due to its emphasis on whole, unprocessed foods and healthy fats.
5. Better gut health: The Mediterranean diet has been associated with a healthier gut microbiome, which can improve digestion, immune function, and overall health.
6. Reduced risk of type 2 diabetes: The Mediterranean diet has been shown to improve insulin sensitivity and reduce the risk of type 2 diabetes, possibly due to its high content of fiber and healthy fats.

7. Longer lifespan: The Mediterranean diet has been associated with a longer lifespan and reduced risk of premature death, possibly due to its anti-inflammatory and antioxidant properties.

Overall, the Mediterranean diet is a healthy and balanced way of eating that can provide numerous health benefits. Its emphasis on whole, unprocessed foods and healthy fats, along with social and cultural practices related to food, make it a sustainable and enjoyable way to improve overall health and well-being.

Meal Planning

A meal plan is a well-organized approach to healthy eating, which involves deciding ahead of time what you will eat for each meal and snack throughout the day. Meal planning can help you maintain a balanced and nutritious diet, while also saving time and money.

The benefits of meal planning are numerous. For starters, it can help you stay on track with your health and fitness goals, as you will be less likely to make unhealthy food choices when you have a plan in place. Additionally, meal planning can save you time and money by reducing the need to make multiple trips to the grocery store or dine out at restaurants.

To create a meal plan, start by deciding on the number of meals you will eat each day. Most people eat three main meals (breakfast, lunch, and dinner) and two snacks, although some may prefer to have smaller, more frequent meals throughout the day.

Next, consider your dietary needs and preferences. For example, if you are trying to lose weight or build muscle, you may need to adjust your caloric intake and macronutrient ratios accordingly. If you have specific dietary restrictions or preferences, such as vegan or gluten-free, make sure to factor those into your meal plan as well.

Once you have an idea of the number of meals you will eat and your dietary needs and preferences, it's time to start planning out your meals. You can do this in a variety of ways, depending on what works best for you.

One popular method is to use a meal planning app or website. These tools typically allow you to search for recipes based on your dietary preferences and create a meal plan for the week. They may also generate a shopping list for you, making it easy to pick up everything you need at the grocery store.

Another option is to create a meal plan on your own using a spreadsheet or notebook. Start by listing out the days of the week, and then plan out each meal and snack for each day. Don't forget to include any leftovers or pre-made meals that you plan to eat throughout the week.

When creating your meal plan, aim to include a variety of foods from all food groups. This will help ensure that you are getting all the nutrients your body needs to stay healthy. Include plenty of fruits and vegetables, lean protein sources, and complete grains in your diet.

Finally, make sure to review your meal plan regularly and make adjustments as needed. Life is unpredictable, and there may be days when you need to switch things up due to unexpected events or changes in your schedule. Flexibility is key to sticking to your meal plan over the long term.

Meal planning is an excellent way to maintain a healthy and nutritious diet, while also saving time and money. By planning out your meals ahead of time and sticking to your plan as much as possible, you can ensure that you are fueling your body with the nutrients it needs to thrive. So why not give it a try and see how it can improve your health and well-being?

Chapter Two

How to Start a Mediterranean Diet Meal Plan

The Mediterranean diet is known for its health benefits and has become increasingly popular in recent years. It emphasizes whole foods such as fruits, vegetables, whole grains, legumes, and healthy fats, such as olive oil, nuts, and fish. If you're interested in starting a Mediterranean diet meal plan, here are some steps to get you started:

1. Learn the basics: Before starting any new diet, it's important to understand the fundamentals. The Mediterranean diet is based on the traditional eating habits of people in countries bordering the Mediterranean Sea. The diet emphasizes plant-based foods, whole grains, healthy fats, and lean proteins.

2. Identify foods to include: To start your meal plan, make a list of foods that fit into the Mediterranean diet. Focus on incorporating plenty of fruits and vegetables, whole grains, nuts, seeds, legumes, and lean proteins such as fish and poultry. Choose healthy fats such as olive oil, avocados, and nuts, and limit or avoid processed foods, refined sugars, and unhealthy fats such as butter and margarine.

3. Plan your meals: Once you've identified the foods to include, plan your meals for the week. Start with breakfast, lunch, and dinner, and include snacks if necessary. Use the Mediterranean diet food list to guide your choices and ensure a variety of nutrient-dense foods.

4. Prepare your meals: Once you have your meal plan, it's time to prepare your meals. This may involve cooking from scratch, batch cooking, or meal prepping for the week. Consider using herbs and spices to flavor your food instead of salt, and experiment with different cooking methods such as grilling, roasting, and baking.

5. Make healthy substitutions: One of the keys to success on the Mediterranean diet is to make healthy substitutions. For example, swap out refined grains for whole grains, use olive oil instead of butter, and choose lean proteins such as fish and poultry over red meat.

6. Practice portion control: While the Mediterranean diet is known for its health benefits, portion control is still important. Pay attention to your portion sizes and aim to eat until you're satisfied, not stuffed.

7. Stay hydrated: Staying hydrated is important for overall health, and it's especially important on the Mediterranean diet. Drink plenty of water throughout the day, and limit or avoid sugary drinks and alcohol.

Starting a Mediterranean diet meal plan can be a great way to improve your health and wellbeing. By following these steps and making healthy choices, you can enjoy the delicious flavors of the Mediterranean while nourishing your body with nutrient-dense foods.

Tips for Planning a Mediterranean Diet Meal Plan

The Mediterranean diet is a popular eating plan based on the traditional foods and lifestyle of countries bordering the Mediterranean Sea. It emphasizes whole, plant-based foods, healthy fats, and lean proteins while limiting processed and refined foods. Here are some tips for planning a Mediterranean diet meal plan:

1. Include a variety of vegetables: Vegetables are a staple of the Mediterranean diet and should be the base of every meal. Aim for a colorful mix of fresh, seasonal produce such as leafy greens, tomatoes, peppers, eggplants, zucchini, and artichokes.

2. Incorporate healthy fats: The Mediterranean diet is high in healthy fats from sources such as olive oil, nuts, seeds, and fatty fish.

These fats can aid in the reduction of inflammation and the promotion of heart health. Use olive oil as your main cooking oil, add nuts and seeds to salads, and enjoy fatty fish such as salmon or mackerel a few times a week.

3. Choose whole grains: Whole grains are a good source of fiber and can help keep you full and satisfied. Opt for whole grain bread, pasta, and rice, as well as ancient grains such as quinoa, farro, and bulgur.

4. Include lean proteins: While the Mediterranean diet is plant-based, it also includes lean proteins such as poultry, fish, and legumes. Aim to include a variety of protein sources in your meals, such as grilled chicken or fish, lentil soup, or chickpea salad.

5. Use herbs and spices: The Mediterranean diet is flavorful thanks to the use of herbs and spices. Try incorporating fresh herbs such as basil, parsley, and mint, as well as spices like garlic, cumin, and turmeric to add flavor to your meals without relying on salt.

6. Enjoy fruits for dessert: Rather than reaching for processed sweets, enjoy fresh fruits for dessert. The Mediterranean diet emphasizes seasonal fruits such as grapes, figs, and pomegranates, which are packed with antioxidants and natural sweetness.

7. Make it a lifestyle: The Mediterranean diet is more than just a meal plan – it's a way of life that includes regular physical activity, socializing, and enjoying meals with family and friends. Incorporate these lifestyle factors into your routine to fully embrace the Mediterranean way of living.

By following these tips, you can create a healthy and delicious Mediterranean diet meal plan that nourishes your body and satisfies your taste buds.

Kitchen Essentials for Mediterranean Diet Cooking

The Mediterranean diet is a popular way of eating that emphasizes whole, minimally processed foods and healthy fats like olive oil and nuts. If you're interested in adopting a Mediterranean-style diet, it's important to have a few key kitchen essentials on hand to help you prepare and cook meals.

Here are some essential kitchen tools and ingredients to consider when cooking Mediterranean-style:

1. Olive oil: Olive oil is a staple of Mediterranean cuisine, so it's important to have a good quality extra virgin olive oil on hand. It's perfect for drizzling over salads, vegetables, and meats, and can also be used for cooking and baking.

2. Herbs and spices: Mediterranean cuisine relies heavily on herbs and spices for flavor. Some essential herbs and spices include oregano, basil, thyme, rosemary, garlic, and cumin. You can use them to season meats, fish, vegetables, and sauces.

3. Grains: Grains like quinoa, brown rice, and whole wheat pasta are important staples of a Mediterranean-style diet. They're great sources of fiber and complex carbohydrates and can be used in a variety of dishes, such as salads, soups, and stir-fries.

4. Fresh produce: Fresh fruits and vegetables are the backbone of the Mediterranean diet. You'll want to keep a variety of colorful produce on hand, including tomatoes, cucumbers, bell peppers, onions, eggplant, zucchini, lemons, and oranges.

5. Seafood: Seafood, particularly oily fish like salmon, tuna, and sardines, are a key component of the Mediterranean diet. They're rich in healthy fats and omega-3 fatty acids, which have been shown to promote heart health.

6. Poultry and lean meats: While the Mediterranean diet is primarily plant-based, it does include some poultry and lean meats like

chicken, turkey, and lean cuts of beef and pork. These can be used in a variety of dishes like stews, kebabs, and salads.

7. Non-dairy alternatives: While dairy is not a major component of the Mediterranean diet, you may want to have some non-dairy alternatives on hand like almond milk or coconut milk. These can be used in cooking or to make smoothies and other beverages.

8. Cooking tools: To prepare Mediterranean-style meals, you'll need some basic cooking tools like a chef's knife, cutting board, vegetable peeler, and colander. You may also want to invest in a good quality grill pan or cast iron skillet for cooking meats and vegetables.

By keeping these essential kitchen tools and ingredients on hand, you'll be well-prepared to cook delicious and healthy Mediterranean-style meals at home.

Grocery List for Mediterranean Diet Meal Plan

A Mediterranean diet is based on the traditional cuisine and eating habits of countries bordering the Mediterranean Sea, such as Greece, Italy, and Spain. This diet emphasizes plant-based foods, whole grains, lean proteins, and healthy fats, and is associated with many health benefits, including a reduced risk of heart disease and stroke.

To follow a Mediterranean diet, here is a grocery list that can help you plan your meals:

- Fresh fruits: Apples, bananas, oranges, pears, berries, melons, and grapes.
- Fresh vegetables: Leafy greens such as spinach and kale, broccoli, cauliflower, zucchini, bell peppers, eggplant, tomatoes, onions, garlic, and carrots.
- Whole grains: Brown rice, quinoa, whole-wheat pasta, whole-grain bread, and oats.

- Legumes: Chickpeas, lentils, kidney beans, black beans, and cannellini beans.
- Nuts and seeds: Almonds, walnuts, pistachios, sunflower seeds, and pumpkin seeds.
- Olive oil: Use this as your main source of fat for cooking and salad dressings.
- Fish and seafood: Salmon, tuna, sardines, shrimp, and scallops.
- Lean meats: Skinless chicken breasts, turkey, and lean cuts of beef and pork.
- Dairy products: Greek yogurt, feta cheese, and Parmesan cheese.
- Herbs and spices: Basil, oregano, thyme, rosemary, cumin, paprika, and cinnamon.

With these ingredients, you can create a variety of delicious and healthy meals, such as grilled fish with roasted vegetables, quinoa and black bean salad, whole-wheat pasta with tomato sauce and vegetables, and Greek yogurt with fruit and nuts. Remember to focus on whole, minimally processed foods and to limit your intake of red meat, sugar, and refined carbohydrates.

Chapter Three

14-Day Mediterranean Diet Meal Plan

A 14-day Mediterranean diet meal plan can help you kick-start your journey to healthy eating. This meal plan is designed to provide you with a variety of nutritious and delicious meals that are rich in fruits, vegetables, whole grains, lean proteins, and healthy fats.

Day 1:

- Breakfast: Berry and almond-topped Greek yogurt
- Snack: Carrots and hummus
- Lunch: Grilled chicken salad with mixed greens, tomatoes, cucumber, and feta cheese
- Snack: Apple slices with almond butter
- Dinner: brown rice, roasted veggies, and baked salmon

Day 2:

- Breakfast: Cinnamon with sliced bananas in your oatmeal
- Snack: Pear slices with walnuts
- Lunch: Mediterranean-style tuna salad with mixed greens, olives, cherry tomatoes, and feta cheese
- Snack: Greek yogurt with honey and walnuts
- Dinner: Grilled chicken with lemon and herbs, roasted sweet potatoes, and steamed broccoli

Day 3:

- Breakfast: fried egg on whole-wheat bread with avocado
- Snack: Mixed nuts and dried fruit
- Lunch: Quinoa and black bean salad with mixed greens, cherry tomatoes, and a lemon vinaigrette dressing

- Snack: Apple slices with cheese
- Dinner: Baked cod with tomato and olive sauce, roasted vegetables, and quinoa

Day 4:

- Breakfast: Spinach and feta omelet with whole-wheat toast
- Snack: Hummus and vegetable sticks
- Lunch: Mediterranean-style chicken and vegetable skewers with a Greek salad
- Snack: Fresh fruit salad
- Dinner: Lentil soup with a side of whole-grain bread

Day 5:

- Breakfast: Greek yogurt with honey, sliced peaches, and granola
- Snack: Trail mix
- Lunch: Whole-grain pita filled with hummus, grilled chicken, and roasted vegetables
- Snack: Apple slices with almond butter
- Dinner: Grilled shrimp with a Greek salad and brown rice

Day 6:

- Breakfast: Fruit and yogurt parfait with granola and honey
- Snack: Mixed nuts and dried fruit
- Lunch: Tomato and mozzarella salad with fresh basil and whole-grain bread
- Snack: Carrots and hummus
- Dinner: Baked chicken with lemon and herbs, roasted vegetables, and quinoa

Day 7:

- Breakfast: Whole-grain toast with scrambled eggs and smoked salmon
- Snack: Pear slices with cheese
- Lunch: Mediterranean-style lentil salad with mixed greens, cherry tomatoes, and feta cheese
- Snack: Greek yogurt, honey, and a variety of nuts
- Dinner: Grilled salmon with a Greek salad and quinoa

Day 8:

- Breakfast: Oatmeal with sliced banana and almonds
- Snack: Fresh fruit salad
- Lunch: Whole-grain pasta with cherry tomatoes, spinach, and feta cheese
- Snack: Hummus and vegetable sticks
- Dinner: Baked chicken with a tomato and olive sauce, roasted vegetables, and brown rice

Day 9:

- Breakfast: Greek yogurt with granola and berries
- Snack: Trail mix
- Lunch: Grilled shrimp salad with mixed greens, cherry tomatoes, and a lemon vinaigrette dressing
- Snack: Apple slices with almond butter
- Dinner: Lentil and vegetable stir-fry with brown rice

Day 10:

- Breakfast: Spinach and feta omelet with whole-grain toast
- Snack: Carrots and hummus
- Lunch: Whole-grain pita filled with hummus, roasted vegetables, and feta cheese

- Snack: Fresh fruit salad
- Dinner: quinoa, roasted veggies, and baked salmon

Day 11:

- Breakfast: fried egg on whole-grain bread with avocado
- Snack: Mixed nuts and dried fruit
- Lunch: Mediterranean-style chicken and vegetable skewers with a Greek salad
- Snack: Pear slices with cheese
- Dinner: Grilled chicken with lemon and herbs, roasted sweet potatoes, and steamed broccoli

Day 12:

- Breakfast: Greek yogurt with honey, sliced peaches, and granola
- Snack: Trail mix
- Lunch: Quinoa and black bean salad with mixed greens, cherry tomatoes, and a lemon vinaigrette dressing
- Snack: Apple slices with almond butter
- Dinner: Baked cod with tomato and olive sauce, roasted vegetables, and brown rice

Day 13:

- Breakfast: Fruit and yogurt parfait with granola and honey
- Snack: Carrots and hummus
- Lunch: Whole-grain pasta with cherry tomatoes, spinach, and feta cheese
- Snack: Greek yogurt, honey, and a variety of nuts
- Dinner: Grilled shrimp with a Greek salad and quinoa

Day 14:

- Breakfast: Oatmeal with sliced banana and almonds
- Snack: Fresh fruit salad
- Lunch: Mediterranean-style lentil salad with mixed greens, cherry tomatoes, and feta cheese
- Snack: Hummus and vegetable sticks
- Dinner: Baked chicken with a tomato and olive sauce, roasted vegetables, and quinoa

Remember, this is just a sample meal plan, and you can modify it to suit your personal tastes and dietary needs. The key is to focus on whole, minimally processed foods and to limit your intake of red meat, sugar, and refined carbohydrates. By following a Mediterranean diet, you can improve your overall health and reduce your risk of chronic diseases.

Chapter Four

Mediterranean Diet Recipes

Breakfast Recipes

Here are ten delicious and healthy Mediterranean diet breakfast recipes with ingredients, instructions, prep time, and serving sizes:

Greek Yogurt and Berry Parfait

Prep time: 5 minutes

Serving size: 1 parfait

Ingredients:

- 1 cup Greek yogurt
- 1/2 cup mixed berries
- 1/4 cup granola
- 1 tbsp honey

Instructions:

1. In a bowl, mix Greek yogurt and honey.
2. Layer the yogurt mixture, mixed berries, and granola in a parfait glass.
3. Repeat the layering until all ingredients are used.
4. Serve immediately.

Shakshuka

Prep time: 15 minutes

Serving size: 2-4 servings

Ingredients:

- 2 tbsp olive oil
- 1 onion, diced
- 2 garlic cloves, minced
- 1 red bell pepper, diced
- 1 tsp paprika
- 1 tsp cumin
- 1/2 tsp salt
- 1/4 tsp black pepper
- 1 can diced tomatoes
- 4 eggs
- 2 tbsp chopped parsley
- Crusty bread, for serving

Instructions:

1. In a skillet over medium heat, heat the olive oil.
2. Add onion and garlic, and sauté for 2-3 minutes until fragrant.
3. Add bell pepper, paprika, cumin, salt, and black pepper, and sauté for another 3-4 minutes until the vegetables are tender.
4. Add diced tomatoes and bring the mixture to a simmer.
5. Use a spoon to create four wells in the mixture, and crack an egg into each well.
6. Cover the skillet and cook for 5-7 minutes until the eggs are set.
7. Sprinkle with chopped parsley and serve with crusty bread.

Avocado Toast with Egg and Tomato

Prep time: 10 minutes

Serving size: 2 servings

Ingredients:

- 2 slices whole-grain bread
- 1 ripe avocado
- 1 small tomato, sliced
- 2 eggs
- Salt and pepper to taste

Instructions:

1. Toast the bread slices.
2. Mash the avocado and spread it evenly on the toast.
3. Top each slice with tomato slices.
4. Fry the eggs to your desired level of doneness.
5. Place an egg on each toast slice.
6. Season with salt and pepper.

Oatmeal with Berries and Almonds

Prep time: 10 minutes

Serving size: 1 serving

Ingredients:

- 1/2 cup old-fashioned oats
- 1 cup almond milk
- 1/2 cup mixed berries
- 2 tbsp sliced almonds
- 1 tbsp honey

Instructions:

1. Combine oats and almond milk in a saucepan and bring to a boil.
2. Reduce heat and simmer for 5-7 minutes until the oats are cooked.
3. Top the oatmeal with mixed berries, sliced almonds, and honey.

Frittata with Spinach and Feta

Prep time: 20 minutes

Serving size: 4 servings

Ingredients:

- 1 tbsp olive oil
- 1 onion, diced
- 2 garlic cloves, minced
- 2 cups fresh spinach, chopped
- 6 eggs
- 1/4 cup crumbled feta cheese
- Salt and pepper to taste

Instructions:

1. Preheat the oven to 350°F.
2. Heat olive oil in a skillet over medium heat.
3. Add onion and garlic, and sauté for 2-3 minutes until fragrant.
4. Add spinach and sauté for another 2-3 minutes until wilted.
5. In a bowl, beat the eggs with salt and pepper.
6. Pour the egg mixture over the spinach mixture in the skillet.
7. Sprinkle feta cheese over the top.
8. Transfer the skillet to the oven and bake for 10-12 minutes until the eggs are set.
9. Slice and serve.

Mediterranean Omelet

Prep time: 10 minutes

Serving size: 1 serving

Ingredients:

- 3 eggs
- 1/2 cup diced tomato
- 1/4 cup diced cucumber
- 1/4 cup crumbled feta cheese
- 1 tbsp chopped fresh parsley
- Salt and pepper to taste

Instructions:

1. In a mixing bowl, combine the eggs, salt, and pepper.
2. Melt butter in a nonstick skillet over medium heat.
3. Pour the egg mixture into the skillet and let it cook for 1-2 minutes until the bottom is set.
4. Sprinkle tomato, cucumber, and feta cheese over one half of the omelet.
5. Fold the other half of the omelet over the filling with a spatula.
6. Cook for another 1-2 minutes until the filling is heated through.
7. Sprinkle with chopped parsley and serve.

Greek Yogurt and Fruit Smoothie

Prep time: 5 minutes

Serving size: 1 serving

Ingredients:

- 1 cup Greek yogurt
- 1 cup mixed frozen fruit

- 1/2 cup almond milk
- 1 tbsp honey

Instructions:

1. Combine all ingredients in a blender.
2. Blend until smooth and creamy.
3. Pour into a glass and serve.

Mediterranean Breakfast Plate

Prep time: 15 minutes

Serving size: 1 serving

Ingredients:

- 2 hard-boiled eggs, sliced
- 1/2 cup cherry tomatoes, halved
- 1/2 cup cucumber slices
- 1/4 cup sliced olives
- 2 slices whole-grain toast
- 1 tbsp olive oil
- Salt and pepper to taste

Instructions:

1. Arrange the sliced eggs, cherry tomatoes, cucumber slices, and olives on a plate.
2. Toast the bread slices and drizzle with olive oil.
3. Season everything with salt and pepper.
4. Serve.

Mediterranean Feta and Spinach Breakfast Wrap

Prep time: 10 minutes

Serving size: 1 serving

Ingredients:

- 1 whole-grain tortilla wrap
- 1/4 cup crumbled feta cheese
- 1/4 cup fresh spinach leaves
- 2 eggs, scrambled
- Salt and pepper to taste

Instructions:

1. Warm up the tortilla wrap in a microwave or on a skillet.
2. Spread crumbled feta cheese on the wrap.
3. Top with fresh spinach leaves.
4. Scramble the eggs with salt and pepper in a skillet.
5. Spoon the scrambled eggs onto the wrap.
6. Fold the wrap over the filling.
7. Serve.

Mediterranean Granola and Yogurt Bowl

Prep time: 5 minutes

Serving size: 1 serving

Ingredients:

- 1/2 cup Greek yogurt
- 1/4 cup granola
- 1/4 cup mixed berries
- 1 tbsp honey

Instructions:

1. In a bowl, mix Greek yogurt and honey.
2. Top with granola and mixed berries.
3. Serve.

Chapter Five

Lunch Recipes

Here are 10 lunch recipes that follow the Mediterranean diet:

Mediterranean Grilled Chicken Salad

Prep Time: 15 minutes

Serving Size: 2

Ingredients:

- 1 lb chicken breast
- 2 cups mixed salad greens
- 1/2 cup cherry tomatoes
- 1/2 cup cucumber slices
- 1/4 cup red onion slices
- 1/4 cup crumbled feta cheese
- 2 tbsp olive oil
- 1 tbsp red wine vinegar
- Salt and pepper to taste

Instructions:

1. Preheat grill to medium-high heat.
2. Season the chicken breast with salt and pepper to taste.
3. Grill chicken for 6-8 minutes per side or until cooked through.
4. In a large bowl, combine salad greens, cherry tomatoes, cucumber slices, and red onion slices.
5. In a separate bowl, whisk together olive oil and red wine vinegar to make the dressing.
6. Slice chicken and add to the salad.

7. Drizzle the dressing over the salad and top with crumbled feta cheese.

Mediterranean Chickpea Salad

Prep Time: 10 minutes

Serving Size: 2

Ingredients:

- 1 can chickpeas, drained and rinsed
- 1/2 cup cherry tomatoes, halved
- 1/2 cup cucumber, diced
- 1/4 cup red onion, diced
- 1/4 cup fresh parsley, chopped
- 2 tbsp olive oil
- 1 tbsp lemon juice
- Salt and pepper to taste

Instructions:

1. In a large bowl, combine chickpeas, cherry tomatoes, cucumber, red onion, and parsley.
2. In a separate bowl, whisk together olive oil, lemon juice, salt, and pepper to make the dressing.
3. Toss the salad with the dressing to coat it.

Mediterranean Tuna Salad

Prep Time: 10 minutes

Serving Size: 2

Ingredients:

- 1 can tuna, drained

- 2 cups mixed salad greens
- 1/2 cup cherry tomatoes, halved
- 1/2 cup cucumber, sliced
- 1/4 cup red onion, sliced
- 1/4 cup pitted and sliced kalamata olives
- 2 tbsp olive oil
- 1 tbsp red wine vinegar
- Salt and pepper to taste

Instructions:

1. In a large bowl, combine tuna, salad greens, cherry tomatoes, cucumber, red onion, and olives.
2. In a separate bowl, whisk together olive oil, red wine vinegar, salt, and pepper to make the dressing.
3. Toss the salad with the dressing to coat it.

Mediterranean Hummus and Vegetable Wrap

Prep Time: 10 minutes

Serving Size: 2

Ingredients:

- 2 large whole wheat tortillas
- 1/2 cup hummus
- 1/2 cup mixed salad greens
- 1/2 cup cucumber, sliced
- 1/4 cup red onion, sliced
- 1/4 cup pitted and sliced kalamata olives
- Salt and pepper to taste

Instructions:

1. Lay out the tortillas and spread hummus on each one.
2. Layer salad greens, cucumber, red onion, and olives on top of the hummus.
3. Season to taste with salt and pepper.
4. Roll up the tortillas and slice in half.

Mediterranean Quinoa Salad

Prep Time: 15 minutes (plus time to cook quinoa)

Serving Size: 2

Ingredients:

- 1 cup quinoa
- 1 can chickpeas, drained and rinsed
- 1/2 cup cherry tomatoes, halved
- 1/2 cup cucumber, diced
- 1/4 cup red onion, diced
- 1/4 cup fresh parsley, chopped
- 2 tbsp olive oil
- 1 tbsp lemon juice
- Salt and pepper to taste

Instructions:

1. Rinse the quinoa and cook it according to package directions.
2. In a large bowl, combine cooked quinoa, chickpeas, cherry tomatoes, cucumber, red onion, and parsley.
3. In a separate bowl, whisk together olive oil, lemon juice, salt, and pepper to make the dressing.
4. Drizzle the dressing over the salad and toss to coat.

Greek Salad with Grilled Shrimp

Prep Time: 15 minutes

Serving Size: 2

Ingredients:

- 1/2 pound large peeled and deveined shrimp
- 2 cups mixed salad greens
- 1/2 cup cherry tomatoes, halved
- 1/2 cup cucumber, sliced
- 1/4 cup red onion, sliced
- 1/4 cup crumbled feta cheese
- 2 tbsp olive oil
- 1 tbsp red wine vinegar
- Salt and pepper to taste

Instructions:

1. Preheat grill to medium-high heat.
2. Season shrimp with salt and pepper.
3. Grill shrimp for 2-3 minutes per side or until cooked through.
4. In a large bowl, combine salad greens, cherry tomatoes, cucumber, and red onion.
5. In a separate bowl, whisk together olive oil and red wine vinegar to make the dressing.
6. Add grilled shrimp to the salad and top with crumbled feta cheese.
7. Toss the salad with the dressing to coat it.

Mediterranean Egg Salad

Prep Time: 10 minutes

Serving Size: 2

Ingredients:

- 4 hard-boiled eggs, peeled and chopped
- 2 cups mixed salad greens
- 1/2 cup cherry tomatoes, halved
- 1/2 cup cucumber, sliced
- 1/4 cup red onion, sliced
- 2 tbsp olive oil
- 1 tbsp red wine vinegar
- Salt and pepper to taste

Instructions:

1. In a large bowl, combine chopped hard-boiled eggs, salad greens, cherry tomatoes, cucumber, and red onion.
2. In a separate bowl, whisk together olive oil, red wine vinegar, salt, and pepper to make the dressing.
3. Toss the salad with the dressing to coat it.

Mediterranean Stuffed Avocado

Prep Time: 15 minutes (plus time to cook quinoa)

Serving Size: 2

Ingredients:

- 1 avocado, halved and pitted
- 1/2 cup cooked quinoa
- 1/2 cup cherry tomatoes, halved

- 1/2 cup cucumber, diced
- 1/4 cup red onion, diced
- 1/4 cup crumbled feta cheese
- 2 tbsp olive oil
- 1 tbsp lemon juice
- Salt and pepper to taste

Instructions:

1. In a large bowl, combine cooked quinoa, cherry tomatoes, cucumber, red onion, and crumbled feta cheese.
2. In a separate bowl, whisk together olive oil, lemon juice, salt, and pepper to make the dressing.
3. Drizzle the dressing over the quinoa salad and toss to coat.
4. Spoon the quinoa salad into the avocado halves.

Falafel Wrap

Prep Time: 10 minutes

Serving Size: 2

Ingredients:

- 4 falafels
- 2 whole wheat tortillas
- 1/2 cup hummus
- 1/4 cup diced cucumber
- 1/4 cup diced tomato
- 1/4 cup diced red onion
- 2 tbsp chopped fresh parsley
- Salt and pepper to taste

Instructions:

1. Cook the falafels according to package directions.
2. Warm the tortillas in the microwave or on a stovetop.
3. Spread hummus on each tortilla.
4. Divide the cooked falafels, diced cucumber, diced tomato, diced red onion, and chopped fresh parsley evenly between the two tortillas.
5. Season with salt and pepper to taste.
6. Roll up the tortillas and serve.

Greek Yogurt Bowl

Prep Time: 5 minutes

Serving Size: 1

Ingredients:

- 1 cup plain Greek yogurt
- 1/2 cup mixed berries
- 1/4 cup granola
- 1 tbsp honey

Instructions:

1. In a bowl, spoon the Greek yogurt.
2. Top with mixed berries and granola.
3. Drizzle with honey.

Note: Serving sizes and prep times are approximate and may vary based on individual preferences and cooking techniques.

Chapter Six

Dinner Recipes

Sure, here are 10 dinner recipes that follow the Mediterranean diet:

Grilled Lemon Chicken Skewers

Prep time: 40 minutes

Serving size: 4

Ingredients:

- 4 chicken breasts, cut into chunks
- 2 lemons, juiced and zested
- 2 tablespoons olive oil
- 2 cloves garlic, minced
- 1 teaspoon dried oregano
- Salt and pepper, to taste

Instructions:

1. In a large bowl, combine the chicken, lemon juice, lemon zest, olive oil, garlic, oregano, salt, and pepper. Allow to simmer for at least 30 minutes.
2. Preheat a grill or grill pan to medium-high heat.
3. Thread the chicken onto skewers and grill for 10-12 minutes, turning occasionally, until fully cooked.

Shrimp and Zucchini Linguine

Prep time: 30 minutes

Serving size: 4

Ingredients:

- 8 ounces linguine
- 1 pound shrimp, peeled and deveined
- 2 zucchini, sliced
- 2 tablespoons olive oil
- 3 cloves garlic, minced
- Salt and pepper, to taste

Instructions:

1. Cook the linguine according to package instructions. Drain and set aside.
2. In a large skillet, heat the olive oil over medium-high heat. Add the shrimp and zucchini, and cook until the shrimp are pink and the zucchini is tender, about 5-7 minutes.
3. Add the garlic and cook for an additional minute.
4. Add the linguine to the skillet and toss to combine.
5. Add salt and pepper to your taste.

Greek Salad with Grilled Chicken

Prep time: 30 minutes

Serving size: 4

Ingredients:

- 4 chicken breasts
- 4 cups mixed greens
- 1 cucumber, diced

- 1 tomato, diced
- 1/2 red onion, thinly sliced
- 1/4 cup kalamata olives
- 1/4 cup crumbled feta cheese
- 1/4 cup red wine vinegar
- 1/4 cup olive oil
- 2 cloves garlic, minced
- 1 teaspoon dried oregano
- Salt and pepper, to taste

Instructions:

1. Heat a grill or grill pan on medium-high.
2. Season the chicken with salt and pepper, and grill for 10-12 minutes, turning occasionally, until fully cooked.
3. In a large bowl, combine the mixed greens, cucumber, tomato, red onion, olives, and feta cheese.
4. In a small bowl, whisk together the red wine vinegar, olive oil, garlic, oregano, salt, and pepper.
5. Toss the salad with the dressing to combine it.
6. Serve the grilled chicken on top of the salad.

Baked Salmon with Lemon and Dill

Prep time: 20 minutes

Serving size: 4

Ingredients:

- 4 salmon fillets
- 2 lemons, sliced
- 4 sprigs fresh dill
- 2 tablespoons olive oil

- Salt and pepper, to taste

Instructions:

1. Preheat the oven to 375°F.
2. Season the salmon fillets with salt and pepper, and place them on a baking sheet.
3. Drizzle the olive oil over the salmon, and place a sprig of dill on each fillet.
4. Top each fillet with a few slices of lemon.
5. Bake in the preheated oven for 12-15 minutes, or until the salmon is fully cooked.

Mediterranean Stuffed Bell Peppers

Prep time: 40 minutes

Serving size: 4

Ingredients:

- 4 bell peppers
- 1 cup cooked brown rice
- 1 can chickpeas, drained and rinsed
- 1 tomato, diced
- 1/2 red onion, diced
- 1/4 cup chopped fresh parsley
- 1/4 cup crumbled feta cheese
- 2 tablespoons olive oil
- 2 cloves garlic, minced
- Salt and pepper, to taste

Instructions:

1. Preheat the oven to 375°F.

2. Remove the seeds and membranes from the bell peppers and cut off the tops.
3. In a large bowl, combine the brown rice, chickpeas, tomato, red onion, parsley, feta cheese, olive oil, garlic, salt, and pepper.
4. Stuff each bell pepper with the rice mixture and place in a baking dish.
5. Bake in the preheated oven for 35-40 minutes, or until the peppers are tender.

Greek Meatballs with Tzatziki Sauce

Prep time: 40 minutes

Serving size: 4

Ingredients:

- 1 pound ground lamb or beef
- 1/2 cup breadcrumbs
- 1/4 cup chopped fresh parsley
- 1/4 cup chopped fresh mint
- 2 cloves garlic, minced
- 1 egg
- Salt and pepper, to taste
- 1 cup plain Greek yogurt
- 1/2 cucumber, grated and drained
- 1 tablespoon lemon juice
- 1 tablespoon chopped fresh dill

Instructions:

1. Preheat the oven to 375°F.
2. In a large bowl, combine the ground meat, breadcrumbs, parsley, mint, garlic, egg, salt, and pepper.

3. Form the mixture into small meatballs and place on a baking sheet.
4. Bake in the preheated oven for 20-25 minutes, or until fully cooked.
5. In a small bowl, combine the Greek yogurt, grated cucumber, lemon juice, dill, salt, and pepper.
6. Serve the meatballs with the tzatziki sauce on the side.

Mediterranean Vegetable Paella

Prep time: 30 minutes

Serving size: 4

Ingredients:

- 1 onion, chopped
- 2 cloves garlic, minced
- 1 red bell pepper, diced
- 1 yellow squash, diced
- 1 zucchini, diced
- 1 cup Arborio rice
- 2 cups vegetable broth
- 1/4 cup chopped fresh parsley
- 1/4 cup chopped fresh basil
- 2 tablespoons olive oil
- Salt and pepper, to taste

Instructions:

1. In a large skillet, heat the olive oil over medium heat.
2. Add the onion and garlic, and cook for about 5 minutes, until they become soft.

3. Add the red bell pepper, yellow squash, and zucchini, and cook until tender, about 10 minutes.
4. . Add the Arborio rice to the skillet and stir to coat with the vegetables and oil.
5. Pour in the vegetable broth and bring to a boil.
6. Reduce the heat to low, cover the skillet, and simmer for 20-25 minutes, or until the rice is tender and the liquid has been absorbed.
7. Stir in the chopped parsley and basil, and season with salt and pepper to taste.

Grilled Chicken Kebabs with Tzatziki Sauce

Prep time: 30 minutes

Serving size: 4

Ingredients:

- 1 pound of boneless, skinless chicken breasts that have been cut into small pieces
- 1 red onion, cut into pieces that are easy to eat
- 1 red bell pepper, cut into pieces that are easy to eat
- 1 yellow bell pepper, cut into bite-sized pieces
- 2 tablespoons olive oil
- 2 teaspoons dried oregano
- 1/2 teaspoon salt
- 1/4 teaspoon black pepper
- 1 cup plain Greek yogurt
- 1/2 cucumber, grated and drained
- 1 tablespoon lemon juice
- 1 tablespoon chopped fresh dill

Instructions:

1. Preheat the grill to medium-high heat.
2. Thread the chicken, red onion, and bell peppers onto skewers.
3. In a small bowl, whisk together the olive oil, oregano, salt, and black pepper.
4. Brush the skewers with the olive oil mixture.
5. Grill the skewers for 10-12 minutes, or until the chicken is fully cooked.
6. In a small bowl, combine the Greek yogurt, grated cucumber, lemon juice, dill, salt, and pepper.
7. Serve the chicken skewers with the tzatziki sauce on the side.

Mediterranean Quinoa Salad

Prep time: 30 minutes

Serving size: 4

Ingredients:

- 1 cup quinoa
- 1 can chickpeas, drained and rinsed
- 1 red bell pepper, diced
- 1/2 red onion, diced
- 1/4 cup chopped fresh parsley
- 1/4 cup chopped fresh mint
- 1/4 cup crumbled feta cheese
- 2 tablespoons olive oil
- 2 tablespoons red wine vinegar
- 1 teaspoon honey
- Salt and pepper, to taste

Instructions:

1. Rinse the quinoa in a fine mesh strainer and add it to a medium saucepan with 2 cups of water.
2. Bring the water to a boil, then reduce the heat to low and simmer for 15 minutes, or until the quinoa is fully cooked.
3. In a large bowl, combine the cooked quinoa, chickpeas, red bell pepper, red onion, parsley, mint, and feta cheese.
4. In a small bowl, whisk together the olive oil, red wine vinegar, honey, salt, and pepper.
5. Pour the dressing over the quinoa salad and mix to coat.

Baked Falafel with Tahini Sauce

Prep time: 30 minutes

Serving size: 4

Ingredients:

- 1 can chickpeas, drained and rinsed
- 1/2 onion, chopped
- 2 cloves garlic, minced
- 1/4 cup chopped fresh parsley
- 1/4 cup chopped fresh cilantro
- 1 teaspoon ground cumin
- 1 teaspoon ground coriander
- 1/2 teaspoon salt
- 1/4 teaspoon black pepper
- 2 tablespoons all-purpose flour
- 2 tablespoons olive oil

Tahini sauce:

- 1/4 cup tahini paste
- 1/4 cup water

- 1 tablespoon lemon juice
- 1 clove garlic, minced
- Salt, to taste

Instructions:

1. Preheat the oven to 375°F (190°C).
2. In a food processor, combine the chickpeas, onion, garlic, parsley, cilantro, cumin, coriander, salt, and black pepper. Pulse the mixture until it is a coarse powder.
3. Add the flour and olive oil to the mixture and pulse until well combined.
4. Form the mixture into small balls, about 1 1/2 inches in diameter, and place them on a baking sheet lined with parchment paper.
5. Bake the falafel for 20-25 minutes, or until golden brown and crispy on the outside.
6. While the falafel is baking, prepare the tahini sauce by whisking together the tahini paste, water, lemon juice, garlic, and salt in a small bowl.
7. Serve the baked falafel hot with the tahini sauce on the side.

Note: The prep time for each recipe is an estimate and may vary based on individual cooking skills and equipment. The serving size is also an estimate and can be adjusted based on personal preference.

Chapter Seven

Snack Recipes

Here are 10 snack recipes for the Mediterranean diet:

Hummus with Carrot Sticks

Prep time: 10 minutes

Serving size: 4

Ingredients:

- 1 can chickpeas, drained and rinsed
- 2 tablespoons tahini
- 2 tablespoons lemon juice
- 1 clove garlic, minced
- 1/4 teaspoon cumin
- 1/4 teaspoon salt
- 2 tablespoons olive oil
- Carrot sticks, for serving

Instructions:

1. In a food processor, combine the chickpeas, tahini, lemon juice, garlic, cumin, salt, and olive oil. Pulse until smooth.
2. Serve the hummus with carrot sticks on the side.

Mediterranean Antipasto Skewers

Prep time: 10 minutes

Serving size: 4

Ingredients:

- Cherry tomatoes

- Mini fresh mozzarella balls
- Artichoke hearts
- Kalamata olives
- Basil leaves
- Balsamic glaze, for drizzling

Instructions:

1. Thread the cherry tomatoes, mini fresh mozzarella balls, artichoke hearts, and kalamata olives onto skewers.
2. Garnish each skewer with a basil leaf.
3. Drizzle the skewers with balsamic glaze before serving.

Greek Yogurt with Honey and Walnuts

Prep time: 5 minutes

Serving size: 1

Ingredients:

- Plain Greek yogurt
- Honey
- Chopped walnuts

Instructions:

1. Spoon the Greek yogurt into a bowl.
2. Drizzle honey over the top of the yogurt.
3. Sprinkle chopped walnuts on top.

Roasted Red Pepper and Feta Dip

Prep time: 10 minutes

Serving size: 4

Ingredients:

- 1 cup of chopped, drained roasted red peppers
- 1/2 cup crumbled feta cheese
- 2 tablespoons chopped fresh parsley
- 2 tablespoons olive oil
- 1 clove garlic, minced
- Salt and pepper, to taste
- Pita chips, for serving

Instructions:

1. In a food processor, combine the roasted red peppers, feta cheese, parsley, olive oil, garlic, salt, and pepper. Pulse until smooth.
2. Serve the dip with pita chips on the side.

Tomato and Basil Bruschetta

Prep time: 15 minutes

Serving size: 4

Ingredients:

- 1 baguette, sliced into 1/2-inch-thick pieces
- 2 cups chopped tomatoes
- 1/4 cup chopped fresh basil
- 1 clove garlic, minced
- 2 tablespoons olive oil
- Salt and pepper, to taste

Instructions:

1. Preheat the oven to 375°F (190°C).
2. Place the baguette slices on a baking sheet and bake for 5-7 minutes, or until lightly toasted.
3. In a bowl, combine the chopped tomatoes, basil, garlic, olive oil, salt, and pepper.
4. Spread the tomato mixture on the slices of toasted baguette.

Spicy Roasted Chickpeas

Prep time: 5 minutes

Serving size: 4

Ingredients:

- 1 can chickpeas, drained and rinsed
- 1 tablespoon olive oil
- 1/2 teaspoon smoked paprika
- 1/4 teaspoon cayenne pepper
- 1/4 teaspoon garlic powder
- Salt and pepper, to taste

Instructions:

1. Preheat the oven to 400°F (200°C).
2. In a bowl, toss the chickpeas with the olive oil, smoked paprika, cayenne pepper, garlic powder, salt, and pepper.
3. Spread the chickpeas in a single layer on a baking sheet.
4. Roast for 20-25 minutes, or until the bacon is crispy.

Caprese Salad Skewers

Prep time: 10 minutes

Serving size: 4

Ingredients:

- Cherry tomatoes
- Mini fresh mozzarella balls
- Basil leaves
- Balsamic glaze, for drizzling

Instructions:

1. Thread the cherry tomatoes and mini fresh mozzarella balls onto skewers.
2. Garnish each skewer with a basil leaf.
3. Drizzle the skewers with balsamic glaze before serving.

Greek Salad Stuffed Cucumbers

Prep time: 15 minutes

Serving size: 4

Ingredients:

- 4 mini cucumbers
- 1 cup chopped tomatoes
- 1/2 cup chopped red onion
- 1/2 cup chopped kalamata olives
- 1/2 cup crumbled feta cheese
- 2 tablespoons chopped fresh parsley
- 2 tablespoons olive oil
- 1 tablespoon red wine vinegar

- Salt and pepper, to taste

Instructions:

1. Slice off the ends of the cucumbers and cut them in half lengthwise.
2. Use a spoon to scoop out the seeds and create a hollow center in each cucumber half.
3. In a bowl, combine the chopped tomatoes, red onion, kalamata olives, feta cheese, parsley, olive oil, red wine vinegar, salt, and pepper.
4. Spoon the salad mixture into the cucumber halves.

Tzatziki with Pita Chips

Prep time: 10 minutes

Serving size: 4

Ingredients:

- 1 cup plain Greek yogurt
- 1/2 cup grated cucumber, drained
- 1 clove garlic, minced
- 2 tablespoons chopped fresh dill
- 2 tablespoons olive oil
- Salt and pepper, to taste
- Pita chips, for serving

Instructions:

1. In a bowl, combine the Greek yogurt, grated cucumber, garlic, dill, olive oil, salt, and pepper.
2. Serve the tzatziki with pita chips on the side.

Roasted Eggplant Dip

Prep time: 10 minutes (plus 45-50 minutes for roasting the eggplants)

Serving size: 4

Ingredients:

- 2 eggplants
- 2 tablespoons tahini
- 2 tablespoons lemon juice
- 1 clove garlic, minced
- 2 tablespoons olive oil
- Salt and pepper, to taste
- Pita chips, for serving

Instructions:

1. Preheat the oven to 400°F (200°C).
2. With a fork, pierce the eggplants all over.
3. Place the eggplants on a baking sheet and roast for 45-50 minutes, or until they are tender and the skin is charred.
4. Let the eggplants cool, then peel off the charred skin and discard.
5. In a food processor or blender, combine the roasted eggplant, tahini, lemon juice, garlic, olive oil, salt, and pepper.
6. Process until smooth and creamy.
7. Serve the dip with pita chips on the side.

Note: serving sizes may vary depending on personal preferences and the number of people being served.

Chapter Eight

Dessert Recipes

Here are 10 dessert recipes for a Mediterranean diet:

Greek Yogurt with Honey and Walnuts

Prep Time: 5 minutes

Serving Size: 1

Ingredients:

- 1 cup Greek yogurt
- 2 tbsp honey
- 1/4 cup chopped walnuts

Instructions:

1. In a small bowl, mix together the Greek yogurt and honey.
2. Top with chopped walnuts.
3. Serve immediately.

Almond and Orange Flourless Cake

Prep Time: 15 minutes

Cook Time: 35-40 minutes

Serving Size: 8-10

Ingredients:

- 3 oranges
- 6 eggs
- 1 cup almond flour
- 1/2 cup honey
- 1 tsp baking powder

Instructions:

1. Preheat the oven to 350°F.
2. Cut the oranges into small pieces, removing the seeds.
3. In a food processor, blend the oranges until smooth.
4. Add the eggs, almond flour, honey, and baking powder. Blend until well combined.
5. Put the batter in a cake pan that has been greased.
6. Bake for 35-40 minutes or until a toothpick inserted into the center comes out clean.
7. Let the cake cool before serving.

Pistachio and Fig Biscotti

Prep Time: 20 minutes

Cook Time: 35-45 minutes

Serving Size: 16-20

Ingredients:

- 1/2 cup unsalted butter
- 1/2 cup sugar
- 2 eggs
- 2 cups flour
- 1 tsp baking powder
- 1/4 tsp salt
- 1/2 cup chopped dried figs
- 1/2 cup chopped pistachios

Instructions:

1. Preheat the oven to 350°F.
2. In a large mixing bowl, cream together the butter and sugar.

3. Beat in the eggs, one at a time.
4. In a separate bowl, mix together the flour, baking powder, and salt.
5. Gradually add the dry ingredients to the wet ingredients, mixing well.
6. Stir in the chopped figs and pistachios.
7. Form the dough into a log and place on a baking sheet lined with parchment paper.
8. Bake for 25-30 minutes or until golden brown.
9. Let the biscotti cool for 10 minutes before slicing.
10. Lay the slices on their sides and bake for an additional 10-15 minutes or until crispy.
11. Let the biscotti cool completely before serving.

Date and Almond Truffles

Prep Time: 15 minutes

Serving Size: 12-16

Ingredients:

- 1 cup pitted dates
- 1/2 cup almond flour
- 1/4 cup cocoa powder
- 1/4 cup almond butter
- 1 tsp vanilla extract
- 1/4 tsp salt
- 1/4 cup chopped almonds, for coating

Instructions:

1. In a food processor, blend together the dates, almond flour, cocoa powder, almond butter, vanilla extract, and salt until well combined.
2. Form the mixture into small balls.
3. Roll the balls in the chopped almonds to coat.
4. Store the truffles in an airtight container in the refrigerator until ready to serve.

Greek Rice Pudding

Prep Time: 5 minutes

Cook Time: 1 hour

Serving Size: 6-8

Ingredients:

- 1 cup short-grain white rice
- 2 cups water
- 4 cups milk
- 1/2 cup sugar
- 1 cinnamon stick
- 1 tsp vanilla extract

Instructions:

1. In a large pot, combine the rice and water. Put on high heat and bring to a boil.
2. Reduce the heat to low, cover the pot, and let the rice simmer for 15-20 minutes or until tender and most of the water has been absorbed.
3. Add the milk, sugar, and cinnamon stick to the pot.
4. Bring the mixture to a simmer over medium heat, stirring frequently.

5. Reduce the heat to low and let the pudding simmer for 30-40 minutes or until thick and creamy, stirring occasionally.
6. Take the pot off the stove and add the vanilla extract.
7. Remove the cinnamon stick and discard.
8. Wait a few minutes to serve the pudding after letting it cool down.
9. Serve warm or chilled.

Lemon Olive Oil Cake

Prep Time: 15 minutes

Cook Time: 30-35 minutes

Serving Size: 8-10

Ingredients:

- 1 cup all-purpose flour
- 1 tsp baking powder
- 1/2 tsp salt
- 2 eggs
- 3/4 cup sugar
- 1/2 cup extra-virgin olive oil
- 1/4 cup freshly squeezed lemon juice
- 1 tbsp lemon zest

Instructions:

1. Preheat the oven to 350°F.
2. Grease a 9-inch cake pan with olive oil and flour.
3. Whisk the flour, baking powder, and salt together in a medium bowl.
4. Beat the eggs and sugar in a separate bowl until they are light and fluffy.

5. Gradually add the olive oil, lemon juice, and lemon zest to the egg mixture, beating until well combined.
6. Mix the dry and wet ingredients together until they are just combined.
7. Pour the batter into the cake pan that has been set up.
8. Bake for 30–35 minutes, or until a toothpick inserted in the middle comes out clean.
9. Let the cake cool before serving.

Orange and Almond Cake

Prep Time: 15 minutes

Cook Time: 35-40 minutes

Serving Size: 8-10

Ingredients:

- 3 oranges
- 6 eggs
- 1 cup almond flour
- 1/2 cup sugar
- 1 tsp baking powder

Instructions:

1. Preheat the oven to 350°F.
2. Cut the oranges into small pieces, removing the seeds.
3. In a food processor, blend the oranges until smooth.
4. Add the eggs, almond flour, sugar, and baking powder. Blend until well combined.
5. Put the batter in a cake pan that has been greased.
6. Bake for 35-40 minutes or until a toothpick inserted into the center comes out clean.

7. Let the cake cool before serving.

Honey and Ricotta Tart

Prep Time: 10 minutes

Cook Time: 25-30 minutes

Serving Size: 8-10

Ingredients:

- 1 sheet puff pastry, thawed
- 1 cup ricotta cheese
- 1/4 cup honey
- 1 egg
- 1 tsp vanilla extract

Instructions:

1. Preheat the oven to 400°F.
2. On a lightly floured surface, roll out the puff pastry.
3. Transfer the pastry to a greased tart pan, trimming any excess pastry from the edges.
4. In a medium bowl, whisk together the ricotta cheese, honey, egg, and vanilla extract until well combined.
5. Fill the pastry shell with the ricotta mixture.
6. Bake for 25-30 minutes or until the pastry is golden brown and the filling is set.
7. Let the tart cool before serving.

Yogurt and Honey Panna Cotta

Prep Time: 10 minutes

Cook Time: 5 minutes

Chill Time: 2 hours

Serving Size: 6-8

Ingredients:

- 2 cups plain Greek yogurt
- 1 cup heavy cream
- 1/4 cup honey
- 1 tsp vanilla extract
- 2 tsp gelatin
- 2 tbsp water

Instructions:

1. In a medium saucepan, heat the heavy cream, honey, and vanilla extract over low heat until just warm.
2. In a small bowl, sprinkle the gelatin over the water and let it soften for 5 minutes.
3. Add the gelatin mixture to the warm cream mixture and whisk until well combined.
4. Remove the saucepan from the heat and whisk in the Greek yogurt.
5. Divide the mixture evenly among 6-8 ramekins or glasses.
6. Chill the panna cotta in the refrigerator for at least 2 hours or until set.
7. Serve chilled.

Fig and Almond Frangipane Tart

Prep Time: 15 minutes

Cook Time: 25-30 minutes

Serving Size: 8-10

Ingredients:

- 1 sheet puff pastry, thawed
- 1/2 cup almond flour
- 1/4 cup sugar
- 1/4 cup unsalted butter, softened
- 1 egg
- 6-8 fresh figs, sliced

Instructions:

1. Preheat the oven to 375°F.
2. On a lightly floured surface, roll out the puff pastry.
3. Transfer the pastry to a greased tart pan, trimming any excess pastry from the edges.
4. In a medium bowl, cream together the almond flour, sugar, and butter until light and fluffy.
5. Add the egg to the almond mixture and beat until well combined.
6. Spread the almond mixture evenly over the pastry shell.
7. Arrange the fig slices over the top of the almond mixture.
8. Bake for 25-30 minutes or until the pastry is golden brown and the filling is set.
9. Let the tart cool before serving.

Note: All recipes can be adjusted to taste and preference. Enjoy!

Frequently Asked Questions

What foods are allowed on a Mediterranean diet?

The Mediterranean diet emphasizes a variety of whole foods, including fruits, vegetables, whole grains, legumes, nuts, seeds, fish, and healthy fats such as olive oil. Red meat is limited, and instead, the diet emphasizes poultry, eggs, and dairy products like cheese and yogurt. Herbs and spices are used to add flavor, and moderate amounts of wine can be consumed.

Is the Mediterranean diet good for weight loss?

Yes, the Mediterranean diet is considered an effective and sustainable approach to weight loss. The diet focuses on whole, nutrient-dense foods and promotes a balanced intake of macronutrients. Studies have shown that the Mediterranean diet can lead to significant weight loss and improvements in metabolic health.

Can I eat pasta on the Mediterranean diet?

Yes, pasta can be included in a Mediterranean diet. However, it is recommended to choose whole grain pasta and to consume it in moderation, as the diet emphasizes a variety of whole foods.

What are some Mediterranean diet snacks?

Some Mediterranean diet snacks include:

- Fresh fruit or dried fruit
- Nuts or seeds
- Hummus or other bean dip with vegetables or whole grain crackers
- Greek yogurt with berries and honey
- Olives and cheese

- Roasted chickpeas or edamame

Is the Mediterranean diet expensive?

While the Mediterranean diet can include some pricier items like fish and nuts, it is generally considered an affordable and accessible way of eating. The diet emphasizes whole, unprocessed foods, which can be purchased at reasonable prices. In fact, some research suggests that the Mediterranean diet may be a cost-effective way to improve overall health and prevent chronic diseases.

Conclusion

The Mediterranean diet is a healthy eating pattern that has been shown to have numerous health benefits. It is characterized by a high consumption of fruits, vegetables, whole grains, legumes, nuts, and healthy fats, such as olive oil and fatty fish. The diet also includes moderate amounts of dairy and red wine, while limiting intake of processed and red meats, sweets, and refined grains.

Studies have found that adherence to the Mediterranean diet is associated with a reduced risk of many chronic diseases, including heart disease, type 2 diabetes, and certain cancers. The diet has also been shown to improve cognitive function and reduce the risk of depression.

One of the key benefits of the Mediterranean diet is its emphasis on whole, nutrient-dense foods. By focusing on fresh produce, whole grains, and healthy fats, individuals following the diet are more likely to meet their nutrient needs and maintain a healthy weight. The diet is also relatively easy to follow, as it does not require strict calorie counting or macronutrient tracking.

Another advantage of the Mediterranean diet is its flexibility. While there are general guidelines for the types of foods to consume and limit, individuals can personalize the diet to their preferences and cultural traditions. For example, a vegetarian or vegan can still follow the Mediterranean diet by focusing on plant-based protein sources, such as legumes and nuts.

It is important to note that the Mediterranean diet is just one aspect of a healthy lifestyle. Regular physical activity, stress management, and adequate sleep are also crucial for overall health and well-being. Additionally, while the diet has many health benefits, it may not be appropriate for everyone. Individuals with certain medical conditions or dietary restrictions should speak with a healthcare professional before starting the diet.

The Mediterranean diet is a healthy and sustainable way of eating that can provide numerous health benefits. Its emphasis on whole, nutrient-dense foods and flexibility make it a practical and enjoyable approach to healthy eating. Incorporating the principles of the Mediterranean diet into your lifestyle can improve your health and overall quality of life.

Printed in Great Britain
by Amazon